Christmastime

Dear S.

Love,
R.

THE LORE
& LEGENDS
OF FLOWERS

THE LORE
& LEGENDS
OF FLOWERS

Robert L. Crowell

Illustrated by

Anne Ophelia Dowden

THOMAS Y. CROWELL   NEW YORK

The author would like to thank the Library of the New York Horticultural Society and the Biblioteca Pública de San Miguel de Allende, Mexico, for their assistance, and Dr. Peter K. Nelson of Brooklyn College and Mary Virginia Harris of The University Museum of the University of Pennsylvania for their helpful suggestions on the manuscript.

The artist wishes to thank the many people who provided both invaluable information and plant specimens to paint. She is particularly indebted to the following: at the Brooklyn Botanic Garden, Dr. Stephen K.-M. Tim, Mr. Edmond Moulin, Mrs. Nancy Shopis Tim, Mr. Frederick McGourty; in Hanover, New Hampshire, Prof. Frederick Page, members of the Hanover Garden Club, especially Mr. and Mrs. Baxter Prescott and Mrs. Betty Sherrard; in Lyme, New Hampshire, Mrs. Erica Parmi.

All plants pictured in this book are exactly natural size.

Library of Congress Cataloging in Publication Data
Crowell, Robert L.
The lore and legends of flowers.
Includes index.
SUMMARY: *Presents lore and legends behind*
several common flowers including narcissus, crocus,
dandelion, carnation, and marigold.
1. Flower language—Juvenile literature.
2. Plant lore—Juvenile literature.
[1. Flower language. 2. Plant lore]
I. Dowden, Anne Ophelia Todd, 1907–   II. Title.
GR780.C76   398'.368213   79-7829
ISBN *0-690-03991-3   0-690-04035-0 (lb. bdg.)*
10   9   8   7   6   5   4   3   2   1
FIRST EDITION

For Muriel,
who loves flowers, too.

Contents

Introduction   I

TULIPS   4

TULIP   *Tulipa gesneriana*

NARCISSI   12

DAFFODIL   *Narcissus pseudo-narcissus*

JONQUIL   *Narcissus jonquilla*

NARCISSUS $\begin{cases} Narcissus\ poeticus \\ Narcissus\ tazetta \end{cases}$

CROCUSES   20

SAFFRON CROCUS   *Crocus sativus*

IRISES   27

BEARDED IRIS   *Iris germanica*

WATER IRIS   *Iris pseudacorus*

CARNATIONS   35

CARNATION   *Dianthus caryophyllus*

GILLYFLOWER   *Dianthus caryophyllus*

PINK   { *Dianthus caryophyllus*
         Dianthus plumarius

ROSES   41

APOTHECARY'S ROSE   *Rosa gallica*

CABBAGE ROSE   *Rosa centifolia*

DAMASK ROSE   *Rosa damascena*

EUROPEAN WILD ROSE   *Rosa canina*

PERSIAN YELLOW ROSE   *Rosa foetida persiana*

NASTURTIUMS   52

NASTURTIUM   *Tropaeolum majus*

DANDELIONS   57

DANDELION   *Taraxacum officinale*

MARIGOLDS   63

AFRICAN MARIGOLD   *Tagetes erecta*

FRENCH MARIGOLD   *Tagetes patula*

POT MARIGOLD   *Calendula officinalis*

DAHLIAS   71

BUSH DAHLIA   *Dahlia pinnata*

SINGLE-FLOWERED DAHLIA   *Dahlia coccinea*

Index   78

Introduction

Further, God said,
"See, I give you all the seed-bearing
plants that are found all over the earth . . ."
Genesis I: 29

A garden full of flowers is a garden full of history, legends, and lore. Every plant could tell a story of where it came from, how it traveled to other parts of the world, how it got its names, and how long it has been cultivated.

Some of our old favorites are as old as civilization. Five thousand years ago the rose flourished in the gardens of China; the Madonna Lily in the gardens of western Asia. And nobody knows how early the doughty dandelion started its journey from central Asia around the world—ubiquitous and unwanted. These and other flowers—and weeds—came to Europe with the westward sweep of civilization, where they joined the snapdragon, the lily-of-the-valley, and dozens of other European natives. Later, after the age of exploration began in the fifteenth century, exotic immigrants were brought from the new lands, such as the dahlia and marigold from Mexico; the nasturtium, zinnia and petunia from South America; and the geranium, gladiolus, and red-hot-poker from Africa. Gradually the four corners of the map were ransacked for flowers that were beautiful or useful or both.

Indeed, flowering plants have been prized for much besides beauty. From earliest times lily bulbs were grown in Asia for food; in the fifth century B.C. the Greeks had a word for "an omelet made of lilies"; and for three thousand years the autumn crocus has been prized as a source of saffron. During the Middle Ages lily petals were used in cooking, violets were chopped up with the onions, and dried calendula petals slightly enlivened the inveterate vegetable stews.

Sometimes the very same flower that was used for food in the kitchen was used in the apothecary shop as a medicine, for nearly every common plant has at some time or other been pressed into service to cure one or more common complaints. And the range of efficacy for a single remedy could be astonishing. According to one authority iris root would cure coughs and colds, stomach pains, women's fomentations, sciatica, fistulas, tumors or ulcers, broken bones, headache—and would cause freckles and sunburn to vanish! Such remarkable powers were often reflected in the names that flowers bore: boneset (for mending broken bones); fleabane (for killing fleas, of course); feverfew (for driving away fever).

Other flowers have quaint or beautiful names because of a fancied resemblance to a buttercup . . . a shepherd's purse . . . or a lady's slipper. Still other names come right out of legend . . . like the name of that lovely little flower that covers swampy spots with a blue mist in the springtime. The story goes that once upon a time a knight and his lady were walking along a riverbank. He was intent upon picking these little blue blossoms for her, when unfortunately he fell in. The current was sweeping him away to his death, but with great presence of mind he tossed the bouquet to his love and cried, "Forget-me-not."

Flowers have been clothed with legends and history in every age and every country. In ancient Greece, Chiron, the centaur, cured his arrow wound with the bachelor's button, which was used medicinally thereafter until well into the nineteenth century. In the Bible the child Moses was hidden away in an ark of "bulrushes," which were most likely the stalks of the graceful papyrus. In an Iroquois legend five chiefs wearing scarlet shirts and yellow moccasins were magically transformed into the wild American columbine.

And just as flowers have flourished in legend it was natural that they should gather symbolic significance to stand for ideas and ideals that mankind has cherished. The ingenuous pansy was called in rural England by such humble names as kiss-me-at-the-garden-gate and three-faces-under-a-hood, but in the Middle Ages it had been symbolic of the Trinity for having three different colors in one blossom. And because pansy comes from the French *pensée*, meaning "thought," the name was considered in the language of love to be an oblique reference to thinking of one's beloved. Some flowers have been used symbolically in different ways in many different religions. The rose was sacred to the Greek god, Dionysus, famous for revelry, and to the Roman goddess, Venus, famous for carnal love. Later it was sacred to the Virgin Mary and was embodied in the rosary.

All flowers are beautiful and interesting, but they are all the more interesting because of the history, the legends, the lore, the literature and the symbolism that surround them.

TULIPS

TULIP *Tulipa gesneriana*

The tulip, one of the great glories of the spring season, is, comparatively speaking, a newcomer to the Western World. It originated ages ago in the Orient, but it did not arrive in Europe until the mid-1500s.

Wild tulips grow—sparingly to be sure—from Japan westward, all across Asia. They prosper in Persia, the Caucasus, Armenia, around the northern shores of the eastern Mediterranean, and even in North Africa. A Minoan jar dating back perhaps four thousand years portrays white tulips on a black background.

In Persia the tulip was a symbol of love, and a legend was told of a young man who committed suicide on hearing the false report that his beloved had died. Where the drops of his blood had fallen, tulip flowers sprang up.

The word *tulip* gives us a clue as to where in the Orient this flower first grew. The Persian word for sash is *dülband*, and it also means "turban"—a sash wound around the head. In colloquial Turkish, the word becomes *tülbend*, which has come to mean "white tulip" because that is what a white turban looks like. From here it was an easy step to the Early Dutch *tulipa*, the Early French *tulipan*, and the modern French *tulipe*.

Many of our garden flowers were born in central Asia, emigrated to the eastern Mediterranean, were adopted by the Greeks and then the Romans, and eventually made their way to western Europe. The tulip, however, remained in what is now Turkey until it was transplanted to western Europe in the sixteenth century. It is not mentioned in classical literature at all, and what may be the first medieval record is a piece of ninth-century Byzantine fabric. There, among the flowers that adorn the border, are—unmistakably—six tulips.

Some seven hundred years later the tulip was brought to Vienna by a colorful gentleman named Ghislain de Busbecq. He was King Ferdinand I's ambassador to the sultan's court in Constantinople. (At the time, King Ferdinand was trying to hold together the Austrian duchies and other portions of his brother Charles V's Holy Roman Empire.) In a letter dated 1556 he wrote home that near Adrianople he had seen "quantities of flowers—narcissi, hyacinths, and tulipans, as the Turks call them." The sultan, he said, had even given him a quantity of tulip bulbs as a token of his esteem for the Austrian ambassador—who rather spoiled the story by adding that he, de Busbecq, had had to give some money for them. At any rate, we know for a fact that de Busbecq sent or

Hybrid Tulips

Broken Tulips

and goose dung. Now, at last, the secret is known: "breaking" was caused by an aphid-borne virus disease that had suddenly struck the tulip bulbs of the East. But of course all variations in the characteristics of tulip flowers are not the result of virus infection. Many of the varieties we now enjoy are the result of careful selection and years of patient hybridization.

In 1634, just a few years after the Pilgrims left Holland, the bulb market went crazy. Even people who didn't know a thing about tulips were buying and selling them like mad: butchers, cobblers, weavers. Bulbs that were still in the ground were traded; bulbs that did not even exist were traded. Tulipomania, as the disease was called, had Holland in its grip.

The most expensive variety of all was the *Semper Augustus*, of which there were said to be only twelve bulbs in existence in 1634. That year, one single bulb sold for 5,500 florins, or about $2,500. Another went for less, 4,600 florins, but the seller had to throw in his carriage with two fine horses.

Three years later, the frenzy subsided. The period had been disastrous for many speculators, but in that short time the tulip achieved enormous favor and prominence all over Europe—a prominence it richly deserved, and one that has grown with the centuries.

NARCISSI

DAFFODIL *Narcissus pseudo-narcissus*

JONQUIL *Narcissus jonquilla*

NARCISSUS $\begin{cases} Narcissus\ poeticus \\ Narcissus\ tazetta \end{cases}$

The narcissus has led a kind of double life. It has been both praised by poets and regarded as sinister in the annals of mythology and in the minds of men. In fact, the bulbs are poisonous; mice and moles eschew them, and as a consequence their lovely, persistent flowers multiply in our gardens year after year.

Until recently people actually believed that the heavy fragrance of narcissus would put you into a coma if you breathed it too long and too deeply. Indeed, according to Pliny the Elder, a Roman naturalist, the very name is derived from the Greek word *narké*, meaning torpor, from which we get our word *narcotic*.

Probably the narcissus that Homer wrote about in his "Hymn to Demeter" was the kind with paper-white bunched blossoms now called *Narcissus tazetta* or "little cup," whose homeland was doubtless Greece or western Asia. This same narcissus has been found entwined in the funeral wreath discovered on Egyptian mummies of the eighteenth dynasty (around 1570 B.C.), but, alas, we have no other clues from ancient Egypt about its age and origin.

The early importance of the narcissus in Greek mythology appears in the rape of Persephone as related by Hesiod. It seems that Zeus had a grudge against Persephone and wanted to help Pluto carry her off. So he ordered the production of a brand-new flower to attract and distract her. That flower was the narcissus. Everything went according to plan. Eros sent a love dart into the susceptible heart of Pluto, who grabbed Persephone just as she was reaching for one of the new flowers. He dragged her into his chariot and headed for the underworld. Right then and there the narcissus grew a little cup in its center to catch Persephone's tears.

The most famous narcissus myth is, of course, the story of the boy Narcissus himself. He went out hunting one day and leaned over a mountain pool to take a drink. There he saw the reflection of his own beautiful face, and he became so infatuated that he lay down by the pool and could not tear himself away. He died there, and was turned into the narcissus flower. Now a person who is overly concerned with his own image is known as *narcissistic.*

There are many strains of native narcissus, and their hybrid descendants have greatly swelled the number. To add to the confusion, there is confusion in the terms! The daffodil, the jonquil, and the narcissus are all kinds of narcissus and are within the meaning of the Latin term *narcissi,* but not everyone knows where one leaves off and the others begin. To add to the confusion, narcissus is a common name for one of the kinds of narcissus! For the

Daffodil

sake of convenience, here are three very broad categories:

1) The daffodil or trumpet type—this includes *Narcissus pseudo-narcissus* and is recognized by its big central trumpet, which is like the mouthpiece of an old-fashioned telephone. It is the parent of almost all of our big-trumpet daffodils.

2) The jonquil, which is yellow but sports different hues of yellow from those of the daffodil. The jonquil has rushlike leaves, and the flowers are clustered on each stem.

3) The narcissus, which has white petals and sepals and a cup often edged with orange or red.

Within these large categories the species and varieties are legion. The "common" daffodil (*Narcissus pseudo-narcissus*), which delighted Wordsworth and which enlivens the window boxes of London each April, is found among trees and in thickets in many parts of northern Europe. The "hoop petticoat" narcissus, with its crown flared out like the skirt of a ballet dancer, makes its home in southern France and Morocco. *Narcissus tazetta*, the most widely distributed of all, is especially partial to Eurasia and the Canary Islands. *Narcissus jonquilla* is native to southern Europe and Algeria. Indeed, the Iberian peninsula is a stronghold of many species that survive in the wild.

One species grows wild even on the remote French island of Réunion, which is situated in the Indian Ocean hundreds of miles from land. There the mountains rise to heights of eight and ten thousand feet, and on the steep upland slopes the narcissus grows wild, but the flowers are few and hard to find. Each spring the children of Lozere, a tiny mountain hamlet, go out to gather the yellow-and-white flowers, which are used in the manufacture of fine perfumes. This precious harvest of blossoms amounts to only about two hundred pounds in all—probably the smallest in the world.

As early as 1627, John Parkinson had distinguished nearly eighty different varieties of narcissus, but in later years many of these disappeared, and for some unaccountable reason narcissus culture suffered a decline for the next two hundred and fifty years. But for the great nurseryman Peter Barr, in England, we might now have far fewer varieties, and the early spring blaze of yellow and gold might be dimmer indeed. Mr. Barr was a Scot who spoke no foreign language and had such a thick burr that his own grandchildren could hardly understand what he was talking about. But nothing fazed Peter Barr. He was determined to collect the narcissi where they grew wild. Beginning in 1887 he made trips to Portugal, Spain, and France, often traveling on horseback or muleback, though he had never ridden before. He went high up in the Pyrenees, and at seven thousand feet found Parkinson's *Narcissus moschatus*, which had disappeared from England by 1629. Looking, looking, digging, digging, he went deep down into mountain valleys, and on one occasion, at least, he slept outdoors under a rock ledge.

Barr could not talk with the people he met, so wherever he went he showed large pictures of the flowers he was looking for. This worked, for he tells of finding six thousand bulbs here, seven thousand bulbs there, and one big haul of nearly twelve thousand.

They were promptly bagged and sent back to England (and eventually replaced by nature, let us hope).

Eager to learn about the bulbs and flowers of other countries, Barr undertook a five-year tour of the world at the age of seventy-two. He traveled to the United States, where he talked with Luther Burbank, the Wizard of Agriculture, in California. He visited growers and nurserymen in Japan, China, Australia, New Zealand, and many islands of the Pacific, and spent six months in South Africa. Everywhere he went he was hailed as the Daffodil King, and everywhere he stimulated excitement and learning about his favorite flower. He was a king indeed, and our gardens owe him a great debt in the spring of each year.

Narcissus tazetta

Jonquil

CROCUSES

SAFFRON CROCUS *Crocus sativus*

Of all the cultivated flowers, the saffron, or autumn-blooming, crocus has one of the longest, most glamorous histories. As a source of saffron it was treasured by ancient kings. In the Middle Ages, a few saffron crocus bulbs would serve as loan collateral instead of jewels. Saffron has been used to raise the spirits of the melancholy, to inhibit intoxication, and to cure the aftereffects of too much drinking. It has been a dye, a medicine, a perfume, and a food flavoring.

The saffron crocus has a purple flower with an orange-yellow center. It blooms only in the autumn; it is not the crocus that blooms so early in the year to tell us that spring is on the way. That is the spring crocus, which may be purple, yellow, or white.

What has made the saffron crocus so highly prized for four thousand years or more is its orange-yellow stigmas. When dried, they constitute the saffron. But to make one ounce of saffron takes the stigmas from about forty-four hundred flowers! Saffron is still sold for cooking, but it is costly and is used sparingly.

Saffron was so highly regarded in most early civilizations that we can fairly well follow its course down through the centuries and around the map. Its homeland was undoubtedly Asia, most likely northeast Iran and Afghanistan. It was known to the Mongols, who may have brought it to the Chinese; early historical records describe oriental robes that were saffron-dyed. Certainly it prospered in Asia Minor, and Corcyrus (now Korghoz) in Cilicia was a great center for crocus culture. The plant was cultivated in Persia; in Kashmir, saffron was the private monopoly of the rajah.

In the eastern Mediterranean countries crocuses were used as decorative motifs as early as 2000 B.C. A four-thousand-year-old pottery jug found at Vasiliki is ornamented with a chain of crocus flowers, quite possibly of the saffron variety. A fresco called "The Blue Boy Picking Crocus" (c. 1900–1700 B.C.), in the great Palace of Minos, at Knossos, Crete, is a lovely portrayal of a person gathering crocus blossoms. And about 1200 B.C. a Greek potter turned out a bowl that was decorated with three crocus blossoms and six slender leaves. It was found on an island off the southern tip of the Greek mainland where the city of Kea stood, now a famous archaelogical dig.

A poet in Solomon's kingdom wrote of saffron in these beautiful and sensuous lines:

Thy plants are an orchard of pomegranates
  with pleasant fruits;
  camphire with spikenard.
Spikenard and saffron; calamus and cinnamon;
  with all trees of frankincense;
myrrh and aloes,
  with all the chief spices.

In Athens crocuses grew in the flower gardens, and saffron was

strewn upon the floors of Greek courts, theaters, and other public buildings to perfume these places. Saffron dye was much sought after in ancient Greece, and the orangey yellow it produced was the stylish color for the robes of upper-class women until the prostitutes adopted it as well. Then styles changed at once.

The Romans went all out for saffron. During Nero's time, they fairly drenched their theaters and banquet halls with it. Between the courses of one of their famous dinners, wrote Petronius, slaves sprinkled the floor with a mixture of sawdust, saffron, vermilion,

Water Iris

IRISES

BEARDED IRIS *Iris germanica*

WATER IRIS *Iris pseudacorus*

The mechanisms by which flowers fertilize one another are many and mysterious. The foxglove keeps its pollen in the finger ends, into which the bumblebee must force its way. Its seeds are tiny, and thousands of them, dropping to the ground at the base of one plant, may never sprout into new life. The dandelion, on the other hand, is a bright and open flower, inviting a visit from any passing insect. Its seeds, equipped with parachutes, can fly on the wings of the wind for hundreds of feet, and take possession of any hospitable spot in which to grow. Hermann J. Muller, an American geneticist, had the theory that blossoms that hold their nectar more deeply develop intricate mechanisms of scent and color to attract the winged creatures that fertilize them.

The pollination machinery of the common bearded iris leaves one full of wonder for its design. By means of its shape, color, and nectar, this iris induces the bee not only to bring it fertilizing pollen from a previously visited iris plant, but to take away some of its pollen to the next—thus enabling itself and its neighbors to reproduce themselves.

After a season of glorious bloom, the petals of the iris fall, and, if the flower has been pollinated, heavy seedpods form where the flower used to be. As the summer wears on, the pods harden and eventually release their seeds. These are large and heavy, and remain where they fall.

The iris has another effective mode of reproduction: the creeping rhizome. The rhizome is a fleshy underground stem at the base of the stalk. (It is sometimes called a bulb, sometimes a root, but both terms are wrong.) From the rhizome, which stores up root food, a few stringy roots grow. During the year's growth, the rhizome sends out additional fingers just below the earth's surface: these eventually send up flower stalks. As gardeners will testify, the iris rhizome is virtually indestructible. Throw it on the compost heap and it does not object; it will still send up leaves and perhaps even a stalk with flowers.

Although the iris has two means of self-propagation, it cannot move very far by either one. It stays right where it grows, dropping seeds and sending out more rhizomes, making a denser clump and slowly spreading outward, but never taking up a new position in a different place. In order to reach new locations the iris has to depend on its friends and admirers. Down through the ages, these have not been wanting, and with the help of gardeners and kings the iris has moved halfway around the globe.

Some say that prior to any records we have, the bearded iris (*Iris germanica*) came from Persia. Certainly it is one of the most ancient of cultivated plants—it was domesticated three to four thousand years ago. In the Cretan Palace of Minos, Sir Arthur Evans found a wall painting clearly showing a youth surrounded by irises in full bloom. Possibly they are a stylized version of the *Iris reticulata*, for these were found growing at the site.

It is known that Thutmose III of Egypt, after subduing a sizeable section of Asia Minor, brought back irises and other plants, which were set out in his palace gardens. He even provided a durable caption, carved in stone on one wall of the huge Temple of Amen. It reads in part, "Plants which His Majesty found in Syria." This species of iris has been identified as *Iris oncocyclus*.

The Greeks and Romans decorated their tombs with iris. Similarly, Mohammedans planted it in their cemeteries; they also carried it with them in their sweep across North Africa. Possibly they brought it to the Iberian peninsula during the early Middle Ages.

In the fifth century A.D., Clovis I, king of the Franks, came to power by defeating his enemies and murdering a few of his relatives. Although Clovis married the Christian Clotilda in 493 and had their children baptized, he himself remained a pagan. However, when a big force of hostile Alemanni invaded his territory, Clovis realized that only a miracle could save him and his vastly outnumbered troops. He prayed to the Christian God of his wife. And then he noticed that there were "yellow flags"—that is, water iris—growing in the waters of a bend in the Rhine. That meant that there the river was shallow enough to ford, and he might

Bearded Iris

be able to circumvent the enemy. His stratagem worked: the Alemanni were put to flight—and Clovis was baptized as soon thereafter as possible. The night of the battle Clotilda had a dream suggesting that Clovis would do well to redesign his battle flag, using three yellow iris flowers instead of the three black toads that had always served before. He did so, and declared that the irises symbolized faith, wisdom, and valor. From that time on, King Clovis had victory after victory.

The "yellow flags" that Clovis observed in the nick of time are the very same species of iris (*Iris pseudacorus*) that grows not only in western European waters, but by quiet streams in the English countryside and the beaver ponds of New England.

Six hundred years after Clovis I's reign, Louis VII of France was organizing the Second Crusade to the Holy Land, and, inspired by a vision, he designed a blazon fairly covered with golden iris flowers. Although his crusade was a disaster, his name is now a part of our vocabulary, for his iris emblem became known as the "flower of Louis." In Old French this was *fleur-de-Loÿs*, which became *fleur-de-luce* and finally *fleur-de-lis*.

Many people have wondered why this emblem is called "the lily of France" when it is really an iris. Similarly, why would Shakespeare say in *The Winter's Tale*, "lilies of all kinds; the flow'r-de-luce being one"? The explanation is that the iris was commonly referred to as a lily right up through the seventeenth century and possibly until later, and, for that matter, it was not uncommon to speak of *any* striking flower as a lily.

Indeed, the iris became first a rival and then a substitute for the lily in Flemish and Spanish paintings. The French House of Burgundy carried the iris emblem, and Burgundy had a role in protecting the Flemish painters. So the Flemish masters began to use it to symbolize the Virgin Mary along with Her flower, the lily. Hugo van der Goes of Ghent did this in his great "Adoration of the Shepherds" (which is now in the Uffizi Gallery). There, in the foreground, occupying the same vase, are two red lilies and three *Iris germanica*—one blue and two pure white. Eventually the Flemish painters used the iris alone, without the lily, to symbolize the Virgin.

Now, there was much intercourse between Flanders and Spain, especially after 1506, when the Hapsburgs incorporated Flanders into their empire. There was trade in artworks and merchandise. Apparently the Flanders connection had its effect on the Spanish masters, because they, too, began to portray the iris as an attribute of Mary.

Carnation

CARNATIONS

CARNATION   *Dianthus caryophyllus*

GILLYFLOWER   *Dianthus caryophyllus*

PINK   { *Dianthus caryophyllus*
          Dianthus plumarius

The English have loved their carnations, or gillyflowers, and their pinks for at least eight centuries; and John Parkinson, the botanist, wrote, "Carnations and Gilloflowers bee the chiefest flowers of account in all our English gardens. . . ."

In those centuries long ago the flower must have been different from the carnations we now see in hothouses and gentlemen's buttonholes. To judge from early descriptions it was a small, single, pink or reddish blossom. How different from the lavish specimens of today, so large and double that they resemble small feather dusters! And such colors: white, white dusted with pink, yellow, apricot, salmon, red, scarlet.

What was the fascination of this unassuming flower? It must have been its scent and flavor, because those are what it was prized for all through its early history. For four hundred years the gillyflower was a flavoring for beers, ales, and wines, and it is recorded that Elizabethan gentlemen preferred not to drink wine at all unless it had a few gillyflower petals floating about in it.

Gillyflower means, in effect, "clove flower." The name grew out of the fact that carnations smell like cloves. Now, the flower of the oriental clove tree looks like a little nut, and the Greek *karuophullon* means properly "nut leaf," thence "clove tree." This word, going through Latin, Arabic, and French, came out in modern English as gillyflower. In other words, the carnation *smells* like a clove, and since the clove flower *looks* like a nut, the carnation was given a name suggesting "nut flower" or "clove flower." The carnation was also often called clove gillyflower.

The carnation's early history is hazy. It was mentioned by Theophrastus, one of Aristotle's pupils, in the fourth century B.C. In his *Enquiry into Plants* he calls it an "under shrub," says it is a "coronary plant," and names it Dianthus, or flower of Zeus. It has retained Dianthus as its genus name to this day.

If we are to believe Pliny (which is sometimes risky), the Romans, too, loved the carnation, and liked to weave its spicy, exotic-smelling blossoms into their garlands. The carnation came to Rome by a circuitous route. There is a tradition that it was already flourishing in North Africa at least two thousand years ago. Parts of North Africa were rife with fevers, and the inhabitants devised various concoctions to obtain relief. However, these medicines tasted so bad that they had to be spiced up to be tolerable, and aromatic carnation blossoms were often used to flavor them. Traders carried the plants to Spain, for in hot climates spices and spicelike plants were always in huge demand. In Spain the carnation caught on, and doctors used it enthusiastically. But the doctors made a mistake: they thought carnations supplied the cure, not merely the flavor. When there was a rebellion in the province of Spain and Augustus Caesar sent some troops to put it down, the officers learned about "the great herb" and were much impressed. They brought plants back to Rome, where they became popular for their beauty, their taste, and their fragrance . . . while their imagined medicinal powers were fortunately forgotten.

Then the carnation disappeared from history for at least a thousand years, though there is a legend that it arrived in Britain with the invasion of Julius Caesar (54 B.C.). Supposedly the seeds were imbedded in the mud on the soldiers' boots! But it is more likely that the carnation came to Britain on the heels of another invader, William the Conqueror (1066). It must have reached England soon after the Conquest, for it is generally acknowledged that almost every region of central and southern Europe had a dianthus of some variety by the end of the eleventh century. Undoubtedly carnations were growing in the abbey gardens of Norman monks at this time; the monks used carnations for medicine, for flavoring their wine, and for decorating their altars.

An account of how this flower was brought to France tells us that there was yet another misunderstanding about its medicinal properties. Louis IX of France had received the surprising report that the ruler of Tunis was just waiting for someone to convert him and his followers to Christianity. So Louis decided to organize a crusade (the Eighth), with a stopover in Tunis. There he would perform the conversion, meet his allies from England and Sicily, and then head for the Holy Land. Alas, the report of the infidels' appetite for Christianity was false; the allies never appeared; and the French, beset by pestilence, died by the thousands. And so did poor Louis himself.

Those French who were left wanted to sail for home as soon as they could. They had concluded that the medicine they had been given, made from pink carnations, had, alone, saved them from the pestilence. So they took plants with them to grow as medicinal herbs in their own country. Probably by the time they discovered that carnations were worthless as medicines, the flower was being admired for its beauty and fragrance.

By the fourteenth century the carnation was doubtless planted throughout England and well implanted in the affections of the English people. Chaucer called it "clow gilofre" and wrote about a mock heroic knight named Sir Topaz (who was patterned after Chaucer himself) riding through the Flanders countryside:

> *Ther springen herbes greet and smale,*
> *The licorys and the cetewale.*
> *And many a clow gilofre, . . .*

This means:

> *Large and small herbs are growing,*
> *The licorice and setwall [an East Indian plant]*
> *And many a clove gillyflower, . . .*

Shakespeare called the carnation "gillyvore," and in *The Winter's Tale* the charming Perdita describes the carnations and "streaked gillyvors" as the fairest flowers of late summer.

Edmund Spenser, who was born a decade before Shakespeare, called the flower "coronation," and thus some concluded that *carnation* is a corruption of *coronation* (coming from the Latin *corona*, meaning "crown"). This is incorrect, however. Most likely *carnation* stems from the Latin *carne* (meaning "flesh"),

Pinks

since the flower is pink or flesh-colored.

The pink itself, the carnation's cousin, is a smaller, somewhat more delicate flower, and its foliage masses on the ground beneath the flower stalks. It spread from eastern Europe westward, arriving in western Europe hundreds of years after its cousin.

Now, one would imagine that the name *pink* would come from the color of the flower, as the carnation's name did. But originally the word *pink* was a verb meaning "to cut a hole or eyelet in a garment by way of decoration." Later, it came to mean scalloping the edges of material so that they would not unravel. Thus we have "pinking shears." Look carefully, and you will see that the petals of pinks—and carnations, too—are scalloped, or pinked. Hence the name of the color, pink, came from the name of the plant!

This little flower has achieved an interesting place in European painting. There are pinks in Botticelli's *Spring*, and in Holbein's portrait of the merchant George Gusis there are pinks in a vase next to the subject. As its title states, this flower is also in Van Eyck's *Man with a Pink*. These flowers were not introduced into the paintings just because they looked pretty. By the time these pictures were painted, the pink had become a symbol of marriage and married love, and often newlyweds in pictures were shown carrying pinks in their hands. In fact, there was an old Flemish custom whereby the bride was expected to hide a pink somewhere on her person on her wedding day, and the bridegroom was expected to search her and find it. Without question he always succeeded.

ROSES

APOTHECARY'S ROSE *Rosa gallica*

CABBAGE ROSE *Rosa centifolia*

DAMASK ROSE *Rosa damascena*

EUROPEAN WILD ROSE *Rosa canina*

PERSIAN YELLOW ROSE *Rosa foetida persiana*

Of all the cultivated flowers in the world, the rose has without doubt been the most highly prized. It was grown by the Chinese during the third millennium B.C. We know from a wall painting of about 1550 B.C. that it was esteemed by the Minoans of Crete, and we have reason to believe that the Rose of Four Seasons was growing in the Hanging Gardens of Babylon around 1200 B.C.

In the New World, roses were flourishing when the Spanish arrived in Mexico in the sixteenth century. When the explorer John Charles Frémont was crossing the North American prairie some hundreds of miles west of the Mississippi River, he found patches of abundant wild roses, blooming as though in man-made gardens.

Officially there are about two hundred species of rose in the world, of which thirty-five species are found in North America

Persian Yellow Rose

Cabbage Rose

from Hudson Bay to the Gulf Coast. Some authorities think that in prehistory there was a proto-rose that made its way in one direction to Europe, and in the other to North America. Others think that a number of different forms emerged independently. We shall probably never know the facts about the rose's ancestors.

We do know that practically all the species that grow in our gardens today (not counting climbers, miniatures, and other special hybrids) are descended from exactly four species. The faithful old cabbage rose, originally brought to Europe by the Romans, was remarkable to the ancients because it had many petals; in fact, Pliny wrote in his nature encyclopedia that it had as many as a hundred petals and hence was called *centifolia* ("hundred petals"). In those days, roses bloomed just once a season and then were through until the next year. Growers tried and tried to produce a repeat-flowering species. The breakthrough was achieved by means of an immigrant from China, brought in the ships of the British East India Company on their return voyages. It was the China rose (*Rosa chinensis*) from Canton, and when it was at last crossed successfully with the cabbage rose in 1840, it produced a whole line of hybrid perpetuals—roses that under favorable conditions bloom more or less repeatedly. An even more effective strain, well formed and free-flowering, had begun arriving in England in about 1810. The tea rose (*Rosa odorata*) was so called because its scent was markedly like that of oriental tea chests. Crossed with hybrid perpetuals in 1867, it established a magnificent line of hybrid teas, which dominate our gardens today.

Professional growers had another goal: to produce stable yellows in bright hues. Before 1900 rose flowers were generally red, white, or pink. Such yellows as there were tended to revert to pink. In 1920 a great French rose hybridizer, M. Pernet-Ducher, after making thousands and thousands of crosses, combined a hybrid perpetual with the Persian yellow rose (*Rosa foetida persiana*) and produced Souvenir de Claudius Pernet. (The name is touchingly reminiscent of the grower's son, who died in World War I.) This great rose was the ancestor of all the beautiful, subtle yellow and flame-colored roses that we nowadays take for granted.

Today's elegant, sculpturelike roses have come a long way from the flat, five-petaled dog rose that the Greeks loved so much. Presumably it was the dog rose that covered the Greek island of Rhodes. *Rhodes* means simply roses, and the flowers were said to grow all over the island in such profusion that if the wind was right, sailors at sea would catch their fragrance even before they sighted land.

The rose figured prominently in Greek language and literature. Homer, the first poet of the Western world, speaks vividly of the "early rosy-fingered dawn," and tells us in the *Iliad* that Aphrodite cured Hector's wounds with roses—no mean feat. Later Greek authors developed a rich and sophisticated vocabulary based upon this beloved flower. There were words for rose honey, rose water, and a confection made of roses and quinces. Instead of "bull in a china shop," they said "bear among the roses." In describing a lady, they might say "rosy ankled," "rosy bosomed," or "rosy bottomed" (or perhaps all three).

It was the Romans who really put the rose to work, and most likely they were the first to grow it commercially. They took it to every part of their empire. It was doubtless under Roman auspices that the cabbage rose followed the shipping lanes to North Africa, then Spain, then the south of France, where it made itself at home and was called rose of Provence (*Rosa provincialis*).

Imperial Rome received vast quantities of agricultural products from its southern dominions. Roman Egypt was the rose farm, and descriptions of Cleopatra's palace indicate that the queen always liked to have her floors covered with a few inches of pink petals! The species of rose grown in Egypt, once called *Rosa rubra*, also followed the trade routes to the west, and eventually it reached

the north of France, there to be extensively cultivated and to become the Apothecary's rose (*Rosa gallica*) of the Middle Ages.

Another species grown by the Romans was the damask rose, and one may see it well portrayed in the wall frescoes of Pompeii. The damask rose was grown in quantity in southern Italy. Doubtless this was the flower that graced Nero's famous orgies. The accounts say that Nero would lie on pillows stuffed with rose petals and would wear a garland and a necklace of roses. No wonder "bed of roses" suggests a special kind of luxury! Nero's fountains would be squirting rose water at full blast. Rose petals were strewn everywhere in the banquet hall; a rose garland was suspended from above, and everything that was said or done during the evening was, by Roman "gentlemen's agreement," said to be *sub rosa*, or "under the rose"—that is, in strictest confidence.

By the second century A.D., Christianity was developing vigorously and spreading rapidly throughout the Roman empire. However, the rose did not prosper with it. As the flower sacred to Venus, the goddess of profane love, and to Bacchus, the god of wine and revelry, it was not acceptable to the Church fathers. Nevertheless, Cyprian, protégé of the great African bishop Tertullian, was, in the early third century, preaching to Christians to die for their faith and for their martyrdom so as to qualify in heaven for "the crown of roses."

Gradually, the rose became acceptable as a symbol of holiness. In the twelfth century the great French mystic, Bernard of Clairvaux, characterized the stigmata of Christ as red roses. He also said that the white rose should stand for the Virgin Mary's virginity and love of God, the red rose for Her charity and compassion. In the same century, Saint Dominic happened to be holding a garland of roses in which the red alternated with the white. He thereupon conceived the idea of the Christian rosary, which originated by threading rose hips on a string like beads.

Ultimately the Virgin Mary became known as "the rose"—that is, the Rosa Mystica of the litany—and Dante wrote in his *Paradiso*, "Christ is at once true God and true man, born of that 'Mystical Rose,' the Virgin."

In the thirteenth century, the rose became the symbol of courtly love and passion. One of the "wandering scholars" wrote this charming verse:

Take thou this rose, O rose,
Since love's own flower it is,
And by that rose
That lover captive is.

Despite its universal popularity, the rose has not been truly important—like saffron, for instance—as an element of food flavoring. Only in the Middle East does the bottle of rose water occupy as important a position on the dining table as the ketchup bottle does in American fast-food restaurants. Down through the ages, it has been used in the kitchen only sporadically.

Marcus Apicius, a contemporary of Nero and a famous Roman gourmand, is credited with a recipe for calf's brains in a sauce made with ground-up rose petals. But it was not until the English Restoration, when anybody would try anything, that rose petals came into their own in the kitchen and rose water became a standard ingredient in sweet dishes.

What the people of early times desperately wanted was medicines to cure their aches and relieve their suffering. The rose, like so many other flowers, was forced into service as a medicine and was said to cure every imaginable ill. By the first century A.D., Pliny and Dioscorides had conceived of more than twenty types of disorders that the rose was supposed to cure. In the twelfth century *Macer's Herbal*, a directory of herbs, commended the rose for everything from eye irritations to bowel trouble, and we know that in the Middle Ages *Rosa gallica* was extensively cultivated for use in medicines and cosmetics.

Apothecary's Rose

As the medieval period ripened, medical prescriptions became more complicated, and, if possible, less sensible. One concoction for the common cold consisted of roses as a vehicle carrying pearls, two little pieces of sapphire, and an ounce each of jacinth, carnelian, emeralds, and garnets, together with mace, basil seeds, ginger, cinnamon, spikenard, gold and silver leaves, red coral, amber, and shavings of ivory.

Such prescriptions were pure quackery, of course, yet as recently as the time of Napoleon, *Rosa gallica* was being cultivated near Paris for use in medicines. The town of Provins abounded in apothecary shops, which shipped dried rose petals all over France for the compounding of medicines. Napoleon's medical corps went there for supplies with which to treat the sick and wounded in the armies of the Emperor. It can only make one sad to think of those delirious soldiers in the pesthouses of Egypt and the frozen wastes of Russia being dosed with dried rose petals.

It is ironic that for centuries physicians used the rose to treat their patients without ever hitting on the part of the plant that is beneficial to humans: rose hips. These are the fruit of the plant, and they are very rich in vitamin C. During World War II the English, deprived of many of the foods they normally imported, had to fight the specter of malnutrition that hovered over their children, and one of the chief weapons was rose hips. Rose hips had long been used to make rosaries, and rose petals had been used to make medicines, but nobody in all those generations of suffering and undernourishment had happened to discover that rose hips would bring health.

NASTURTIUMS

NASTURTIUM *Tropaeolum majus*

The flowering of the Renaissance during the last half of the sixteenth century was a golden age for botany. In Spain, France, Flanders, and England botanists were writing, translating, and publishing. Charles de l'Ecluse of Flanders came to England, met with Francis Drake, the first Englishman to circumnavigate the globe, and asked him what plants he had brought back from the New World. Philip II of Spain sent his own physician, Dr. Hernandez Macias, to Mexico for seven years to find out about Aztec pharmaceuticals, and while the Spanish padres taught Christianity to the Indians, they in turn learned about Aztec medicine.

Like good gardeners everywhere, the botanists shared their seeds as well as their knowledge. As the sixteenth century was drawing to a close, John Gerard and John Parkinson, great English botanists, were corresponding with and trading seeds with John Robin in Paris. Meanwhile, Dr. Nicolás Monardes, a physician and scholar in Seville who had a wonderful curiosity about the new discoveries in natural science, was engaging in a spirited correspondence with kindred botanists in both the New World and the Old. He established one of the first museums in Europe, in which he exhibited products of nature that ships brought to Spain in their holds. (Eventually Carolus Linnaeus, a Swedish botanist, named a botanical order after him.) The good doctor wrote a pioneering book that he called *Medicinal history of the things brought from our west Indies* (1574). Mentioned in this book were "Floures of Blood"—nasturtiums—which the doctor had grown from seeds brought him from Peru. Dr. Monardes sent some of his nasturtium seeds to John Robin in France, who sent some to John Gerard in England. There, John Parkinson declared that nasturtiums were without curative value, but they were received with delight and cherished for their beauty.

In the next century, the seventeenth, the nasturtium came into its own as a salad green—and well it might, for a nasturtium leaf contains ten times as much vitamin C as a lettuce leaf the same size. Of course, no one knew this at the time. So when English sailors sought an antidote for the terrible scurvy that was rampant then—and which vitamin C prevents—they used the wrong part of the plant. They pickled nasturtium pods instead of eating the leaves. At last, with the end of the eighteenth century, they learned to fight off scurvy with the lemons and limes that had become available—and therefore came to be called "limeys." The nasturtium as a health food was quietly discarded.

The young flower buds of the nasturtium can be used for a seasoning, the flowers for garnish, the leaves and stems in salads, and the seeds, chopped up, for a condiment. The seedpods, picked green, may be pickled and used instead of capers. Nasturtiums are featured in several famous modern recipes, such as President Dwight D. Eisenhower's vegetable soup recipe and Alice B. Toklas's Turkish salad recipe. And the "sallet" recipe of John Evelyn, a seventeenth-century English country gentleman, sounds as fresh and delicious as ever. He wrote in his "Discourse on Sallets" that a nasturtium "sallet" would contain "the tender leaves, Calices, Cappuchin, Capers and flowers laudably mixed with the colder Plants"; should be "discreetly" sprinkled with spring water; and—this sounds modern enough—"remain a while

in the Cullunder and finally swung together gently in a clean coarse napkin." The dressing sounds even better than the salad: "Oyl without smell or the least touch of rancid . . . the best Wine Vinegar . . . the brightest Bay gray-salt; Mustard; Pepper . . . not bruis'd to too small a Dust; the Yolks of fresh New-laid Eggs, boil'd moderately hard, to be mingl'd and mashed with the Mustard, Oyl and Vinegar" and "the seeds are pounded in a Mortar; or bruis'd with a polished Cannon-Bullet"!

How, one wonders, did a lovely flower from the mountains of Peru take on such a formidable appellation as *nasturtium* for its everyday name? Literally translated from Latin, *nasturtium* means "nose twist," and it could be said that its pungent odor does twist your nose. Some say that the Romans coined this word to designate a certain malodorous cress of theirs, and little by little it attached itself to all cresses, including the innocuous watercress. After the nasturtium reached England, it was regarded as another of many cresses, and was commonly called "Indian cress." That is not what the Spaniards in Peru called it. Their name was *capuchina*, or "little hood," and that is the plant's name all over South America now.

English herbalists like Parkinson, seeing the nasturtium's long spurs, called it "yellow lark's heel." Finally, Linnaeus had another idea. To Linnaeus, the leaves looked like shields, and the blossoms looked like helmets. So he conferred upon the flower already carrying the Latin name *nasturtium* the Latinized scientific name *Tropaeolum*—"of the trophy pillar." This is a rather farfetched reference to the trophy pillar (*tropaeum*) where Roman soldiers hung up the armor taken from slain adversaries.

In its relatively short history the nasturtium has been given many names and has been used in cookery in many ways. In gardens it has been used in different ways, too. It was very popular during the time of Louis XIV, when that monarch's famous landscape architect, Le Nôtre, used it in formal, patterned flower beds. Then, in about 1750, there was a swing back to naturalism, and with this change in style the poor nasturtium was uprooted from geometrical gardens. But it is a lovely, exotic flower, and we prize it for its beauty in our gardens—as John Parkinson did more than three hundred years ago in his.

DANDELIONS

DANDELION   *Taraxacum officinale*

No one knows where the dandelion originated, but it probably was central Asia. The dandelion has been characterized as "the tramp with the golden crown." It springs up in carefully groomed gardens, multiplies by the roadsides, and forces its way through the cracks in city sidewalks. As a persistent weed, it flourishes in every temperate region of the world.

Its name is really a mispronunciation of the French *dent de lion* —"lion's tooth." This has a nice regal sound, but in France the term is rather archaic. The name *pissenlit*—"wet-the-bed"—is now used, and its appears incongruously among the salad selections on French menus.

Opinions vary as to why the plant was called "lion's tooth." Some say that the petals of the golden flowers resemble the teeth of the lion as they appear in heraldry—that is, coats of arms and

Dandelion

the like. Others, with perhaps more plausibility, point to the deep-cut, jagged leaves. Still others say that the root is tooth-shaped.

The reason that dandelions can find so many places to grow is that they have great numbers of seeds and a marvelous seed-distribution system. Starting in the spring, long before many other plants have even flowered, the dandelion blossom rapidly ripens toward maturity; each yellow floret produces a tiny parachute, and to each parachute is attached a seed. Two hundred or more of these filmy, fuzzy parachutes radiate at different angles from the end of each old flower stalk. Together they form a perfect globe, and, as an old French dictionary so charmingly puts it, "The head, when blown upon, vanishes."

Everyone likes to blow on these balls of fuzz and watch the parachutes take off. People have been doing it for generations, and this has given us many old legends and folk beliefs. It is said that if the seeds are blown away by the wind in the early morning, there will be good weather that day. On the other hand, if the seeds leave the stalk without having been blown by the wind, it will rain.

This is how you use a dandelion to tell time: blow the seeds away, counting the number of puffs it takes to dislodge them all. That number is the hour of the day. You can also foretell the future by blowing on the seed head.

If you can blow away all the seeds in three puffs, that means your mother does not want you home. However, if any seeds are left, you'd better run home as fast as you can.

Blow hard with one great big puff; then count the seeds that remain. That is how many children you will have.

If you can blow off all the seeds in one puff, your sweetheart loves you very much. If a few are left, your sweetheart is not faithful. If many are left, your sweetheart is completely indifferent to you.

In Maryland they say that if dandelion blossoms do not open in the morning, rain will come during the day. Wear a dandelion—or just pick one—and you may wet the bed.

At various times the properties of the dandelion have been considered to be numerous and marvelous. The Irish used the dandelion as a tonic and as a cure for heart disease. The juice, rubbed on warts, supposedly caused them to disappear. The English made a concoction from the roots that was supposed to be a spring tonic and was said to purify the blood, benefit the liver, and help with rheumatism. In Silesia it was thought that dandelions picked on Midsummer Eve not only had special medicinal qualities but would ward off witches as well.

Most people do not realize it, but every single part of this "worthless weed" can be used: the leaves, the stems and flowers, and the roots. Quantities of the greens are sold every spring in the markets of Europe, Mexico, New York City, and elsewhere. They are boiled and served as a vegetable, or used raw in salads and soups. For generations youngsters have been told by their mothers to eat the wild dandelion greens on their plates "because they are good for you," and nowadays dandelions are actually cultivated; seedsmen sell the seeds for several dollars an ounce. Indeed, dandelion greens are an important source of vitamin A, and half a cup of them per day will satisfy a person's vitamin A requirements. Sautéed dandelion buds may be used in omelets; the petals in sandwiches; the stems and blossoms for making wine.

Even the dandelion root—that long white ugly root that looks like a shriveled parsnip and oozes a milky white sap—is useful. Roasted, it becomes a kind of imitation coffee that is sometimes a coffee substitute and sometimes is mixed with coffee to "stretch" this costly commodity. The sticky milk that flows from the severed root looks much like the sap from a rubber tree. Well it might, for it contains latex, and from latex rubber can be made. In fact, there is a species of Russian dandelion from which latex has been extracted in commercial quantities. Finally, the root contains a substance that is used as a laxative. Who would think that food, chemical, and medicinal products could all be made from dandelion roots?

As a symbol, this jaunty flower has had some strange and diverse meanings. It has been used to portray grief and bitterness, and early Flemish and German painters used it in pictures of the Crucifixion, and elsewhere, to suggest the suffering of Christ. But it has also symbolized the sun—and, of all things, coquetry. Considering its many uses, perhaps the humble dandelion should be the symbol of versatility!

Pot Marigold

MARIGOLDS

AFRICAN MARIGOLD *Tagetes erecta*

FRENCH MARIGOLD *Tagetes patula*

POT MARIGOLD *Calendula officinalis*

Marigold, meaning Mary's gold, is a beautiful name, and it has been generously bestowed on half a dozen or more flowers, most of which have nothing in common and some of which are not even gold in color. There is the marsh marigold, which Pliny himself confused with the pot marigold. There is the daisylike cape marigold. There is the sea marigold, with white, glistening branches and flowers. There is the corn marigold, native to England. There is the pot marigold, which American gardeners usually call calendula. There is the African marigold, which is not African. And there is the French marigold, which is not French.

The marsh marigold is indigenous to temperate zones in Europe and North America, where it may be seen blooming in the very early spring in a bog, by a swollen brook, or on a riverbank. It is thought to have been growing healthily in the British Isles

French Marigold

The so-called African marigold did not reach Europe from Africa, but came from Mexico very soon after the Spanish conquest. When Cortés invaded Mexico in 1521, he brought soldiers to take the lives of the inhabitants and priests to save their souls. These padres took pains to study the lore and the flora of the New World, and they soon found out about a yellow flower with aromatic leaves that the Aztec priests mixed with tobacco and smoked to produce trances and prophetic visions. The padres sent its seeds

back to Spain, where the plant not only prospered but spread rapidly, even making its way to the North African coast. It was "discovered" all over again in North Africa in 1535 when Emperor Charles V sent over troops to free Tunis from the Turks. Brought back to Europe, it was ceremoniously christened Flos Africanus. It has been called African marigold ever since. Even the scientific name, *Tagetes erecta*, invented two hundred years later, gives no clue to the marigold's Mexican origin. *Tagetes* refers to an Etruscan youth by the name of Tages, who, having learned divination, was murdered, then deified.

The Aztecs were fond of flowers, and flowers were very much a part of their culture. Women wore them in their hair and men carried them in their hands. They revered the African marigold, and most likely used it to honor their dead, for this flower has been known in Mexico as the flower of the dead (*flor del muerto*). In their Nahuatl language (which is still spoken today), the Aztecs called it Cempoalxóchitl, from *cempoalli* (twenty) and *xochitl* (flower)—in English, "twenty flower." It is called Cempasúchil in Mexico to this day, and it grows profusely along the roadsides and in the fields where the corn has been cut. The plant stands two to two and a half feet high and has a single flower (not a double flower like the hybrid species) that from a distance looks something like a large orange-yellow buttercup. In dry weather the foliage seems a bit scraggly compared with the foliage of our pampered garden specimens, but the powerful scent of the leaves is unmistakable. Like most "weeds" and wildflowers, it has little place in the flower markets of its homeland. But on All Souls' Day

(November 2), and on the day or evening that precedes it, this marigold is used, according to the custom in different regions, to decorate the grave or to grace the house during ceremonies to welcome back the soul of a departed member of the family. No doubt the Mexicans honor their dead with African marigolds partly because their Aztec forebears did, but also partly for a practical reason: the fall is the time of year when the flower blooms.

The so-called French marigold (*Tagetes patula*) was sent to Spain from Mexico just as the African marigold was, and it eventually made its way to France. It is supposed to have been brought to England by the Huguenots. In Mexico it is called Cempoalxóchitl (Nahuatl) cimarrón (Spanish), meaning "wild twenty flower," and it grows wild south of Mexico City in the lava formations.

The French marigold is much bushier and much lower in stature than the African marigold. Its flowers vary in color from golden yellow to bloody orange. It, too, has the characteristic marigold odor that used to be such a trial to English gardeners. In fact, there seems to be only one marigold that does not have it, and that is the *Tagetes lucida*, which has a very pleasing, aromatic scent. The Aztecs called it *yyauhtli* and used it to cure hiccups. It is a pity William Hanbury, who wrote in the eighteenth century, did not have it in his garden. As it was, he found nothing good to say about marigolds, and wrote of the African marigold, "These flowers stink as bad, or worse, than the French Marygolds. . . ."

Single-flowered Dahlia

DAHLIAS

BUSH DAHLIA *Dahlia pinnata*

SINGLE-FLOWERED DAHLIA *Dahlia coccinea*

When the Spanish forces under Cortés invaded the lake country of the Aztecs and their neighbors, they were dumfounded by what they saw. It was like enchantment, wrote Cortés's lieutenant Diaz del Castillo, and some of the soldiers wanted to know if they were in a dream. Montezuma II had palaces and gardens such as no prince of Europe could afford: there were aromatic flowers and shrubs, groves of tropical trees, reservoirs for fish and wildfowl, and everywhere terraces, pools, and fountains splashing water. The gardens of Montezuma's brother in nearby Iztapalapan were even more magnificent—here one could see exotic flowers from all over Mexico in scientific arrangements covering a huge area. At Texcoco, Montezuma's cousin Nezahualcóyotl, the poet-king and philosopher, had a palace of three hundred rooms. In his gardens there were labyrinths of shrubbery, baths with fountains and basins, groves of cedar and cypress. Outside the city were his recreation gardens, with shady walks, groves, pools, and baths of great capacity. Sizable aqueducts, together with intricate waterworks, were built to ensure that the gardens were well supplied with water.

But in less than a generation, wrote Díaz, all this splendor was destroyed and the crystal pools were a putrid mess. Now there is nothing left of Nezahualcóyotl's recreation gardens but a few building stones; of Montezuma's imperial gardens there remain a few cypresses.

Some flowers were sacred to the Aztecs and were reserved for the priests. Some, like the magnolia, were the flower pets of royalty. Some were used for food, and the number used as medicines ran into the thousands. We know this because Dr. Ignacio Hernandez Macias, sent over by Philip II of Spain in 1570, recorded some three thousand plants that the Aztecs employed for the relief of human ailments. They treated both the flesh and the mind.

One of the plants that Dr. Hernandez Macias described had an unpretentious flower with eight red rays. The Aztecs called it Acocóxochitl, "the hollow-stem plant," or Acocotli, "water cane." It was an ingredient in their prescription for epilepsy, and it was sacred to their war god, Uitzilopochtli, for the red rays symbolized his thirst for blood. The Spanish doctor had discovered what we call the dahlia, which had been cultivated in Mexico long before the Europeans ever came there, and was one of the favorite flowers of Montezuma and Nezahualcóyotl.

However, the dahlia, which was later to cause a sensation, did not reach Europe until the end of the eighteenth century. The seeds were sent from Mexico to Abbé Cavanilles of the Royal Gardens in Madrid. He was fortunate enough to nurture not one species but three: the bush dahlia (*D. pinnata* syn. *variabilis*), and *D. coccinea* and *D. rosea*. At least that is what we call them now, because the good Abbé, with complete disregard for the exotic origins of this New World flower, conferred upon it a genus name concocted from the last name of Andrew Dahl, a botanist in faraway Sweden. Attempts have been made to change it, but to no avail. It is called *dalia* even in the flower markets of its Mexican homeland.

This new genus soon attracted the interest of aristocratic gardeners in England and France. A Lady Bute sent specimens to England less than a decade after dahlias became established in Spain, but they died. Another unsuccessful attempt to grow dahlias was made by an English nurseryman, whose dull red-brick specimen actually got into *Curtis' Botanical Magazine* of 1803 before it expired. Finally a Lady Holland sent seeds to England in 1804. These sprouted and prospered. Lady Holland's species included the bush dahlia and *Dahlia coccinea*, both of which became exceedingly good parents.

However, before they ever got to England, dahlias were growing in French gardens—quite by accident. The minister from France to Mexico wanted people in his own country to cultivate cochineal insects for their extremely valuable crimson dye. So he approached an impecunious French botanist who happened to be in Mexico at the time, a Nicholas Thierry de Menonville, and asked him to smuggle a supply of the insects out of Mexico and into

Hybrid Dahlias

France. M. Menonville was successful in hiring Indians to collect a good supply for shipment, and quite wisely also asked them what the insects should be fed on the long voyage. "The red-flowered cactus," he was told, but all he understood was "red flower," and he dutifully amassed a supply of nice red dahlias, and threw in some seeds and tubers as well. The insects died of starvation, but the seeds and tubers made the journey safely and added a new and exciting flower to French horticulture.

Dahlias soon came to the attention of none other than Napoleon's wife, Josephine. In her gardens at Malmaison she planted them with her own imperial hands. She even had a dahlia reception to which diplomats and dignitaries were invited so they might regard the splendor of her favorites in bloom. On this august occasion a Polish prince bribed one of Josephine's gardeners to smuggle out a hundred tubers at one louis d'or apiece. Josephine, outraged, never cultivated dahlias again. However, they continued to be very fashionable in France, and by 1826 sixty varieties were known. When their potato crop failed in 1840, the French even experimented with dahlia tubers as a substitute, but the French could not tolerate what the Aztecs had enjoyed.

By the 1870s the Dutch were importing new species, including the lovely cactus dahlia, directly from Mexico, and during the last quarter of the century a kind of dahlia craze swept Europe.

Now, the very remarkable bush dahlia and *Dahlia coccinea* do not hybridize with each other, but individually they possess the most extraordinary and valuable genetic characteristics. While *D. coccinea* refuses to produce double flowers, it is the parent par excellence of the different single-flower varieties—like the eight-rayed Aztec original—that regularly come in and out of fashion. In the hands of modern growers, *D. coccinea* has produced a whole rainbow of brilliantly colored varieties of dahlia: yellows, corals, carmines, and vermilions. They made the dull red of the original look dull indeed.

The bush dahlia has the capacity to produce double flowers, and, oddly enough, this doubling tendency increased after the plant's arrival in Europe. No one knows why. It was named *variabilis* for good reason, because its ability to generate different colors and markings in its offspring surpasses even that of *D. coccinea*. These two species have more capacity for variation than any known flower, including the tulip. In the comparatively short time since the beginning of the nineteenth century, the dahlia family has proliferated to the point where fourteen thousand named varieties have been produced.

When the rains of late summer come to the region south of Mexico City, the months of glory for the native dahlias begin. Growing in wild and radiant profusion by the roadsides and in the fields are the very flowers that were cultivated in Aztec gardens.

Index

"Adoration of the Shepherds" (Goes), 33
African marigolds, 63, 66–69
Apicius, Marcus, 49
Aztec culture, uses of flowers in, 52, 66, 68–69, 71–72, 76

Bacchus, 48
Bacon, Francis, 25
Barr, Peter, 17–18
basil, 3
Bernard of Clairvaux, 48
botany, golden age of, 52–53
Burbank, Luther, 18

cabbage roses, 41, 44, 46
Caesar, Augustus, 37
Caesar, Julius, 37
Calendula officinalis, 63
calendulas (pot marigolds), 3, 63–65
carnations, 35–40: in ancient Rome, 36–37; emigrations of, 36–38; as flavoring, 36–37; as medicine, 37–38; origin of word, 39–40
Cavanilles, Antonio José, 73
Charles V, Holy Roman Emperor, 5, 68
Chaucer, Geoffrey, 38
China roses, 44
Cleopatra, 46
Clotilda, queen of the Franks, 29–32
Clovis I, king of the Franks, 29–32
cochineal insects, 73–76
corn marigolds, 63
Cortés, Hernando, 66, 71
crocuses, 20–25: as decorative motifs, 21; as source of saffron, 20
Crocus sativus, 20
cross-pollination of dandelions, 27; of foxgloves, 27; of irises, 27–28

Curtis' Botanical Magazine, 73
Cyprian, Saint, 48

daffodils, 12–18: confusion about name of, 13–16
Dahl, Andrew, 73
Dahlia coccinea, 71, 73, 76–77
D. pinnata, 71
D. pinnata syn. *variabilis*, 73
D. rosea, 73
dahlias, 71–77: in Aztec culture, 71–72; bush, 71, 73, 76–77; proliferation of, 77; single-flowered, 71
damask roses, 41, 47
dandelions, 27, 57–61: folk beliefs about, 59–60; latex extracted from, 61; in medicine, 60; origin of, 57; origin of name, 57–59; seed distribution of, 59; symbols of, 61; uses of, 60–61
de Busbecq, Ghislain, 5–8
Dianthus, 36
Dianthus caryophyllus, 35
D. plumaris, 35
Díaz del Castillo, Bernal, 71–72
Dioscorides, 2, 49
"Discourse on Sallets" (Evelyn), 54
dittany, 3
Dominic, Saint, 48
Drake, Sir Francis, 52

Eisenhower, Dwight D., 55
Enquiry into Plants (Theophrastus), 36
Eros, 13
Evans, Sir Arthur, 29

Ferdinand I, King, 5–8
fleur-de-lis, origin of, 32
foxgloves, 27

Frémont, John Charles, 41
French marigolds, 63, 69

Galen, 2
garden flowers, emigration of, 5
gardens: Aztec, 76, 77; Elizabethan, 3;
    medieval, 2–3
Gerard, John, 52–53, 65
Gesner, Konrad von, 8
gillyflowers, 35: as flavoring, 36; origin of
    word, 36; in poetry, 38–39
Goes, Hugo van der, 33

Hanbury, William, 69
Henry VIII, king of England, 24, 25
herbs, 3
Hernandez Macias, Dr. Ignacio, 52, 72
Hesiod, 13
Hill, Sir John, 65
Hippocrates, 2
Holbein, Hans, 40
Homer, 12, 45
"Hymn to Demeter" (Homer), 12
hyssop, 3

Iliad (Homer), 45
irises, 27–33: bearded, 27–28, 29; in
    emblems, 32–33; history of, 29–33;
    lilies compared with, 32–33; pollination
    of, 27–28; rhizomes of, 28; as symbol
    of Virgin Mary, 33; water, 27, 29–32
Iris germanica, 27, 29, 33
I. oncocyclus, 29
I. pseudacorus, 27, 32
I. reticulata, 29
iris root (orrisroot), 2

jonquils, 12, 13, 16
Josephine, empress of France, 76

l'Ecluse, Charles de, 8, 52
Le Notre, André, 56

lilies, 3: in Flemish and Spanish art, 33;
    iris as rival of, 32–33
Linnaeus, Carolus, 53, 56
Louis VII, king of France, 32
Louis IX, king of France, 37–38, 56

Macer's Herbal, 49
magnolias, in Aztec culture, 72
Man with a Pink (Van Eyck), 40
marigolds, 63–69: African, 63, 66, 68–
    69; in cooking, 64–65; corn, 63; in
    folk medicine, 65, 66, 68–69; French,
    63, 69; marsh, 63–64; meaning of
    name, 63; pot (calendula), 3, 63–65;
    sea, 63
marjoram, 3
marsh marigolds, 63–64
Medicinal history of the things brought
    from our west Indies (Monardes), 53
Menonville, Nicholas Thierry de, 73–76
mint, 3
Monardes, Dr. Nicolás, 52–53
Montezuma II, 71–72
Muller, Hermann J., 27

narcissi, 12–18: categories of, 16; con-
    fusion about names for, 13–16; in
    Greek mythology, 13; "hoop petti-
    coat," 16; in Lozere, 17; medical
    myths about, 12; in perfumes, 17; va-
    rieties of, 12, 17
Narcissus, myth of, 13
Narcissus jonquilla, 12, 16
N. moschatus, 17
N. poeticus, 12
N. pseudo-narcissus, 12, 16
N. tazetta, 12, 16
nasturtiums, 52–56: origin of word, 55–
    56; regarded as cresses, 56; as salad
    greens, 53–54; as source of vitamin C,
    53
Nero, 47
Nezahualcóyotl, 71–72

oregano, 3
orrisroot (iris root), 2

Paradiso (Dante), 48
Parkinson, John, 9, 17, 35, 52–53, 56
Pernet-Ducher, M., 45
Persephone, 13
Philip II, king of Spain, 52, 72
pinks, 35: in European painting, 40; origin of word, 40; as symbol of marriage, 40
Pliny the Elder, 12, 36, 44, 49, 63
Pluto, 13
pot marigolds (calendulas), 3, 63–65

rhizomes, in iris reproduction, 28
Robin, John, 52–53
Rosa canina, 41
R. centifolia, 41, 44
R. chinensis, 44
R. damascena, 41
R. foetida persiana, 41, 45
R. gallica, 41, 47, 49, 51
R. odorata, 44
R. provincialis, 46
R. rubra, 46–47
Rosa Mystica, 48
rosaries, origin of, 48
rose hips, 48: as source of vitamin C, 51
roses, 41–51: Apothecary's, 41, 47; cabbage, 41, 44, 46; China, 44; in cooking, 49; in cosmetics, 49; damask, 41, 47; dog, 45; esteem of, 41; European wild, 41; in Greek vocabulary, 45; hybridizations of, 44–45; in Imperial Rome, 46–47; in medicine, 49–51; Persian yellow, 41, 45; in Rhodes, 45; species of, 41–44; symbolization of, 48–49; tea, 44
rose water, 45, 49

saffron, 20–25: in cooking, 21, 24–25; crocuses cultivated for, 20, 25; dyes,

saffron (*cont.*)
21, 23–25; history of, 21–25; in medicine, 1, 2, 25; origin of word, 24; in poetry, 21–22; in smallpox epidemics, 1; as treasure, 21–22; uses of, 20–21
saffron crocuses, 20, 25
Saffron Walden, England, crocus production at, 25
scurvy, 53
Sea marigolds, 63
Semper Augustus, 11
Souvenir de Claudius Pernet, 45
Spenser, Edmund, 39
Spring (Botticelli), 40
sub rosa, 48

Tagetes erecta, 63, 68
T. lucida, 69
T. patula, 63, 69
Taraxacum officinale, 57
tea roses, 44
Tertullian, 48
Theophrastus, 36
Thutmose III, king of Egypt, 29
Tropaeolum majus, 52, 56
Tulipa gesneriana, 4, 8
tulipomania, 11
tulips, 4–11, 77: breeder bulbs of, 9; emigrations of, 4–5, 8; fanaticism about, 11; hybridizations of, 9–11; in Low Countries, 8–9; origin of, 4; origin of word, 5; as symbols of love, 4; wild, 4
Turner, William, 25

Uitzilopochtli, 72

Venus, 48
violets, 3

William the Conqueror, 37
Winter's Tale, The (Shakespeare), 32, 39, 64

Zeus, 13